# REMEMBERING
## *Lela & Charlie*
### —The Blue Springs Years—

Written by
## *Mable Elizabeth Gates*

Forward and Book Design by
*Lela Rast Hartsaw*

For questions, further information,
or other inquiries, contact the author:
whatsmamawriting@gmail.com

# Dedication
## by Brenda Dowdy Bell

Duncan Gates
7/19/30 – 6/6/18

This second volume of *Remembering Lela & Charlie* by Aunt Mable is being dedicated to her husband, Duncan. Without his love and devotion none of this would have been possible.

I can almost remember the day when I first met Duncan Gates. I couldn't have been more than three or four years old, but when you meet someone that is "larger than life", you tend to remember.

The first thing one always noticed, apart from his friendliness, was his humor. Life itself was a joy for Duncan. His goal was to share that joy with everyone. He always achieved that goal.

Right up until the end of his life, he would welcome you into his home with a "Get in here; Mable is frying pies" and see you out later with a "God bless you" and "I love you"!

Throughout his life he took care of everyone he possibly could. Pay a light bill if you couldn't or with Mable by his side, bring food, which might be the only meal you'd had in two days.

Later, when his in-laws, Lela & Charlie, could no longer take care of themselves, he prepared a home for them on his property and for ten years he and Mable were their main caregivers.

"Without Duncan I couldn't have taken care of Mama and Daddy," Mable says. "He made sure I always had a car to drive and sometimes worked 10-12 hours a day to make it financially possible for us to do what we had to do."

We love you Uncle Duncan and we miss you so much.

3

# Forward
## by Lela Rast Hartsaw

Reading my Aunt Mable's story, which she had written sometime in the 1980s, about life with my namesake, her mother and my great grandmother, tugged on more than my heartstrings. When I first read this, I was a young professional, working in an ad agency. I was mesmerized by Aunt Mable's storytelling; her ability to paint a picture is truly a gift. As I read, even though her typing had errors and there were some grammatical glitches—all left in this book, as written—I could imagine the story becoming a screenplay and a movie. It felt like a story that belonged on the screen, not because it was overly dramatic or glamorous, but because it was so very *real*. The life story of Lela & Charlie is a snapshot of the American experience. They married just after World War I, raised a young family during the Great Depression, then lived through three more wars— World War II, Korea, and Vietnam—and watched as the world changed with each passing decade. Their children grew into adulthood, some started families of their own, two passed away too soon, and all experienced their fair share of joy and pain.

Aunt Mable documented moments of daily life that my children can barely imagine like doctors making house calls and living in a house with only one electric light bulb. When I read this for the first time, I made a promise that I would edit her work and get it published. It needed to be published. But, life became more complicated for me and at the time, personal computers and the Internet were just becoming a reality. Then I married and started a family and everything else was put on the way back burner.

Until 2017, Aunt Mable's story remained tucked away, a binder-clipped stack of typed pages waiting for the right moment to finally become a more polished, publishable collection. Rather than edit the pages, I found a way to publish her typed manuscript as-is and the effect was marvelous. My mother and daughter contributed to the task, Mom via research and family photos and Emily through providing illustrations, which were remarkable for a girl of thirteen. *Remembering Lela & Charlie—A Four Generation Book Project* was published in

November of 2017, but without the last chapter. We chose, instead, to leave off at Lela & Charlie's 52nd Wedding Anniversary, a very special time in their lives and what seemed to be a happier ending for the book.

What you hold in your hands today is that last chapter which details the years where Lela & Charlie live in a lovely mobile home across the driveway from Aunt Mable and Uncle Duncan, under the tall pines, on beautiful property in Blue Springs. The setting was peaceful, and allowed Aunt Mable to care for her parents in their final years. She carried them to countless doctor's appointments, maintained two houses, and prepared three meals each day for her husband and her parents.

The tales of hospital visits, multiple illnesses, and the sacrifices and compromises that come with elder care almost makes this bittersweet account more like a cautionary tale. My hope is that you'll find the golden nuggets hidden within and cling to them as I do.

*Lelo Hartsaw*

Lela Rast Hartsaw, Author of
*The Adventures of Abigail Rose—Ida Patten's Antebellum Doll*
and *Abigail Rose Visits Gamble Plantation*

# REMEMBERING
## Lela & Charlie
### —The Blue Springs Years—

Mable Elizabeth Gates

# Chapter 1

One day in the Fall of 1973, Charlie called to Elizabeth's house, he wanted to speak to Duncan. He would not tell Elizabeth what he wanted to talk to him about. The first thing he told Duncan was that he did not have a home any more. Duncan did not know what he was talking about. He then asked Duncan if he bought a mobile home could he put it on his place. Duncan could not believe he meant it, but told him he would be glad for him to put it there if that was what he really wanted.

Charlie told him he was going to have to put it somewhere, that he had sold his place to Byron Benefield.

At first Duncan did not believe him, he never thought he would sell his place. When he hung the phone up and told Elizabeth what her father said, she could not believe it, so she called her mother right back and asked if it was really the truth.

Lela said, "Yes, your daddy has sold out, we know we can't keep this place up any longer. We are going to have to get somewhere that some one will help us." Elizabeth said, "I never thought Daddy would sell his place, you know we will do everything we can for you, but it is still a shock."

Charlie and Lela came up that weekend, and wanted Duncan to take them to look at mobile homes. They looked and looked, but did not find anything they liked. He told them they would go and look again.

Christmas came and went, that week they found a mobile home that was suitable for their needs. Duncan got the rock for the septic tank and put it in and when the home was delivered, had it hooked up with all the utilities.

The first day of 1974, they moved in. While they

were gone to get a load of things, Elizabeth had the heat on and things cleaned up and ready to put their clothes and personal things up, she also had a lunch fixed for the movers.

Elizabeth worried about her father, she knew he would not be able to forget his home he had lived in for over fifty years, she was afraid he would be very unhappy.

Lela was sick that week they moved, Elizabeth took her to the Doctor. He told her she needed a lot of rest. So, she brought her home and put her to bed.

For the next few months, that was the way it was, when finally, with rest and good care she began to feel some better.

Tony was in college, and the house was nearly always full of boys. Most of them liked to play cards. They would go at night and play Rook with Charlie.

Mable Elizabeth Gates

# Chapter 2

The last part of 1975, Elizabeth took Charlie to Dr. Pettis in Tupelo to have his eyes examined. He said he had cataracts and had to have an operation.

A few weeks after the surgery, Elizabeth was taking him back to the doctor. She had dressed that day in cotton pants and a pullover sweater.

Charlie was smoking as usual. He had his sack that he carried to spit in sitting near his feet. They were on the four-lane when somehow Charlie caught his paper sack on fire. Elizabeth was horrified when she could look down; her pants leg was blazing. There was no where to stop, or go, finally she got to a wide place on the edge of the pavement and pulled over long enough to beat the flames out and to throw the paper sack out the window.

Wearily she drove on to the doctor's office. Her leg was hurting so bad she could hardly stand to touch it. Finally she found some pins in the car pocket and pinned it together enough so the flesh would not show. She knew she had to take her father into the doctor's office because he could not see well enough to go alone.

She got him registered, and as she started to sit down she noticed one of the society ladies of Tupelo looking at her. She had seen the lady's picture in the paper enough to know who she was.

She turned to the lady and said, "When you were growing up did your father ever tell you he was going to burn your britches for something you had done? Well, I Must have done something wrong because Daddy just almost burned mine off me!"

Strangely, the lady thought that was the funniest thing she had ever heard and wanted to hear all of the story. When they started into the doctor's office, the lady said, "Good luck dear, I'm afraid you will need it, before you get through with all of this." When she got home she put some salve on her burns and bandaged them. They were into blisters by then and really hurting.

It seemed that either Charlie or Lela were sick all the time now. It was as if they had given up and all the fight had gone from them.

Tony had married that year, and they missed him. He had spent a lot of time with them, and was now living in New Albany. That Fall he came out one day and said he was going to join the Air Force. Lela was so sad. Elizabeth told her he was never going to get anywhere working at a convenience store. She pointed out to her that his father and grandfather had both been in the service. All Lela could think of was how much she was going to miss them. Elizabeth had been having lots of problems with her health. That November when she went for her check up, Dr. Thomas told her she had waited as long as she had better wait to have surgery. She asked him to wait till after Christmas. So he set it for January the 7th.

Elizabeth set about cleaning her house good, she even cooked and froze several meals for Bunny the dog, as she wouldn't eat anything but chicken.

Christmas passed all too soon, and it was time for the surgery. Elizabeth thought she had never been so sick. After a week she came home. Lela and Dee cooked and Dee cleaned the house, did the wash, and ran all the errands.

Tony was to leave on the 8th of March. It was a sad day for all of them. Dee was going to spend most of the time with them until she could go to the base where Tony was.

Charlie could not get used to Elizabeth not being able to do what he needed to have done. While she was still in the bed, his check came and he came walking down the hall of her house back to the bedroom where she was resting. He stood in the doorway and said, "Sis, my check has come, I need to go to town." She said, "Daddy, you know I can't drive the car now, but Dee said she would take you to the bank." He looked at her for a long time, then turned around and started back down the hall. Elizabeth heard him talking to himself, "It takes you longer to get well than anybody I know."

# Chapter 3

In May, Tony came home on leave and to get Dee. They were stationed at Sheppard Air Base in Wichita Falls, Texas. After they left everyone was lonesome. Elizabeth kept Shawn most of the time. He liked to stay with them. Lela and Charlie petted him since he was the only small one in the family.

Elizabeth tried to do everything she could to make them happy. She carried them wherever they wanted to go. Lela began to have blackout spells.

She would be standing doing something, and just fall suddenly and be unconscious for several minutes. Elizabeth carried her to the doctor in New Albany, and they sent her to Tupelo to several doctors there. They put her into the hospital and ran all kinds of tests but could not find the problem.

That Christmas, Tony could not get leave to come home. So, he asked his mother and father to come to Texas for Christmas. Before time to go, Lela had a bad spell and fell, breaking some ribs. She was in the hospital for several days. Elizabeth thought she would not go, but she knew Tony would be disappointed, since this was the first Christmas that he had ever been away from home.

She asked Hazel if she and Shawn would come and stay, Elizabeth cooked up some things and froze them so they would have something to eat.

All during Christmas Lela worried about them travelling. She was afraid something would happen while they were gone.

Shortly after the New Year, one morning, Elizabeth went to the door and looked out when she heard what she thought was a dogfight. She saw what looked like several large dogs, and then she saw some of them looked like wolves.

One of them stayed behind when the rest ran into the woods. The large shaggy dog hung around the house all that day. Lela couldn't stand to think of anything being hungry, so she brought a plate of scraps out onto the small back porch. The dog would not come near the food until Lela went into the house. After looking all around, the wolf-like dog slowly climbed the back steps, and in almost one bite ate the whole plate of food. Charlie had always loved dogs, so each day when Lela put the food out, Charlie stood at the back door and watched the dog eat. While he was eating Charlie talked to him in a slow singsong voice. The big dog was still not quite ready to trust anyone to put their hands on him.

That Saturday night, Duncan and Elizabeth went out to eat and to shop in Tupelo. When they returned around nine o'clock, the dog was lying on the top step of the porch of Charlie and Lela's house. When the car stopped, Lela opened the door, and called Elizabeth to come out there when she finished putting away her groceries. As she was walking past the dog later, Elizabeth reached over and scratched the big dog behind the ear. He kept in step with her as she walked the short distance to her parent's house.

Lela wanted to know if they could keep the dog? Elizabeth said, "Yes, we bought feed tonight and we will take him for his shots next week."

From that time on, Jack the dog belonged to all of them, he went with Charlie on his walks each day, and when he got near a place that was not level, Jack would walk almost against his legs, as if to push him over to safer ground.

In March of 1977 it was warm that first week, Ruth had not been well. Elizabeth told her mother that she was going to make Ruth some egg custards and chicken and dumplings and take them to her. By the time she had the food cooked Charlie and Lela were ready to go. When they got there Ruth seemed hungry and ate a lot of the food. She especially enjoyed the pie. She ate half of one of them, she told Elizabeth she believed that was the best one she ever ate. While they were talking, she asked Elizabeth to watch over Pat, her daughter, and help her if she ever could. Elizabeth promised her she would. On the 11th of March they found Ruth dead, she had died in her sleep. Once more Charlie and Lela had to bury one of their children. Lela grieved for Ruth so much. They had always been so close, Lela was just a young girl when Ruth was born, and they always did everything together.

That June Hazel had to have surgery, Elizabeth brought her and Shawn to her house so she could take care of them and still see after Charlie and Lela.

The surgery was worse than the doctor led them to believe, Hazel had not been home a day or two, when Elizabeth heard her calling her one night. By the time she got to the bedroom blood was running off the bed.

She ran to the phone and called the doctor, he told her to get her to the hospital as soon as she could. Hazel was in the hospital several more days, then Elizabeth brought her back home. A few more days passed and the same thing happened again. This time it was in the daytime, so Elizabeth carried her to the doctor's office. He said, "It is a hematoma." He cleaned it out and Elizabeth brought her back home. Lela had kept Shawn, she had him busy building a house with clothespins.

Finally she got some better, but she was not able to go home until the last of August.

In 1978, Hazel bought a mobile home and put it at Duncan and Elizabeth's so Elizabeth could help take care of Shawn and send him to school while his mother worked.

# Chapter 4

Sorrow seemed to come to the family more often. In February of 1979, Pearl's husband Lloyd passed away. Charlie and Lela could not do much for Pearl, so Elizabeth tried to help her in every way she could.

Lela was sick most of the time now, in the Fall of 1979 Dr. Shirley sent her to a neurologist in Tupelo. He put her into the hospital to run tests. She had a roommate, so Elizabeth came home to take care of Shawn and Charlie. They kept her and ran all kinds of tests but they failed to show what was causing the blackouts.

On the morning she was to come home, Elizabeth rose early and cleaned both houses. It was a terrible morning. A cold rain was falling like silvery tears across a gray curtain. She told Charlie she would be back as soon as she could. When she got to the hospital she drove around for what seemed like hours, but there was just no parking space except on the last level. By the time she reached the door she was soaked, she pulled her shoes off and poured the water out of them before she went inside. When she got to her mother's room, it was around eleven. The doctor had not been around, so she had to sit as wet as she was, and wait. She pulled off her shoes and stockings, and hung them over the vent so the heat could dry them as much as possible. By the time she got to the car, she was as wet as she had been when she got inside the hospital. Lela seemed so quiet; Elizabeth asked her if she was feeling worse. Her eyes filled with tears as she said, "I am worse off than you think I am." Elizabeth said, "Well, what do you want to do?" "I don't know what else to do, but I will take you wherever you want to go." Lela said, "I don't know of anything else we can do."

By the time they got home, the rain had slacked some. Elizabeth parked as close to the door as she could. She worried that she might not be able to get Lela inside by herself. She got behind her mother and put both arms under Lela's and pushed her up the steps, into the house.

Once inside, Lela said she had to go to the bathroom. Without thinking, Elizabeth helped her to the toilet and sat her down. She turned to pick up something off the vanity, and just saw her mother as she was falling sideways off the commode. She grabbed her before she completely fell.

She tried everything she knew to revive her, but nothing worked. She finally called Charlie and told him to get a wet rag to wash her face. Elizabeth stood and held her mother until she thought her back would break. She could not turn her loose because she would fall off the toilet.

An hour passed. Finally she heard a car coming up the driveway. She told Charlie to go to the door and tell whomever it was in the car that she needed help. She heard him open the front door, then she heard Duncan talking to Charlie. Duncan came into the bathroom, and Elizabeth asked why he had come home at that time? He told her that he heard her calling him as plain as he had ever heard anything. She said, "It must have been God that called you because I sure was asking him to send me some help."

They pulled the straight chair Lela kept in the bathroom as close to the toilet as they could, Duncan got behind her and Elizabeth got in front and they pulled her onto the chair, then they pulled the chair to the bedroom. Elizabeth spread a clean towel on the bed and when they had rolled her onto it she got a pan of water and cleaned her up. Elizabeth was exhausted by then, she had to sit down and rest for a while before she could fix supper.

Lela continued to have these spells, but no doctor could find the cause.

In January of 1980 Charlie had pneumonia. Dr. Shirley told him to come back for x-rays after he had taken all his medicine. The day was cloudy and very cold. As Dr. Shirley was examining Charlie, Lela fell onto the floor, she had blacked out. The doctor looked at Elizabeth asking her, "Do you have anyone to help you?"

She said, "No, I don't." He left the room and came back with a wheelchair for Lela. He said, "I called Linda to come help you, when you have one lying on the floor and another that can't stand by themselves, it's time for some help."

He wrote orders for Elizabeth to take Lela to the hospital for tests, and x-rays. Linda took Charlie to her house until Elizabeth could get all that done.

When the tests were all done and it was found that she did not have any broken bones, they went to get Charlie so they could go home. As they left New Albany a light rain had begun to fall and the closer they got to home, Elizabeth realized it was freezing. She had never had to drive on ice before, when the car started to slide toward a deep gulley, Lela began to scream, Elizabeth fought the wheel and finally got it straightened back in the road. She said, "Mama, please be quiet, I am so scared and you screaming is making me so nervous, I am afraid I will wreck the car."

They crept and slid until finally they were in the driveway, she was so happy to be off the road she said to Lela, "Now you can scream if you want to." When they were in the house Elizabeth realized she was wet with sweat, her blouse was stuck to her back and water had ran down her arms, she had been so scared she had to rest before she could fix them something to eat.

Pearl came more often, her husband Lloyd had passed away in February of 1979, so she had some time on the weekend that she could help out.

Lela was getting steadily worse. The first of February Lela told Elizabeth she wanted to quilt her mother's old quilt into a new top and bottom. Elizabeth got the material she wanted and they sat at the machine.

Elizabeth sewed and Lela would guide the material through for her. They talked as they worked. Lela said, "I am more sick than you think I am; and I do not believe I will be here much longer." Elizabeth tried to tell her that she would get better, but Lela seemed to know that her time was almost up. Lela kept talking, "I want you to fix my hair when I die if it won't bother you to do it." Elizabeth stopped the machine, and took her mother's hand. "If it will make you feel better, I do promise you that I will fix your hair, it does not matter if it does bother me, I will do it anyway." Tears came in her mother's eyes, "Thank you," she said. "It feels better when you fix it than it does when anyone else does it."

In the following weeks Lela had become much worse, her once clear beautiful skin became yellow, and she was sick to her stomach much of the time. Dr. Shirley did all he could, but she became much worse as the weeks wore on. On the 15th of May Charlie took pneumonia again and had to stay in the hospital. Lela insisted on staying with him. One of the nurse's aids, Amy Keaton, called Elizabeth and told her that Lela had fallen in the bathroom and blacked out.

While Hazel went to the hospital to get Lela, Elizabeth stayed home and cooked all of them something to eat and cleaned the house. When they returned they both realized that something was very wrong with their mother. She seemed dazed and nothing they said to her seemed to sink in.

Lela insisted on going back to the hospital after she had eaten and had a bath. They both begged her to let one of them stay with Charlie, but she would not hear of it and became angry when they kept begging her to stay home and rest. Elizabeth expected the worst, every time the phone rang. Her feelings of unease continued after she brought her father home the next day.

Toward noon that day Elizabeth was getting something together for all of them to eat, the phone rang. It was Pat, telling her that Charlie Howard, Carolyn's son, had been found in the Tombigbee River. His car had gone off the road the night before as he came home from work.

Charlie and Lela were terribly upset over the news. Charlie Howard had always been good to stop and see them and they loved him. He was named for his great grandfather.

That Sunday night Elizabeth was so worried about them that she decided to spend the night with them. When time came to go to bed she told her mother not to get up if Charlie needed anything that she would get it for him.

Sometime after midnight, Elizabeth heard Charlie get up, she was awake and listening to see if he needed anything. She did not want to bother him since she knew how he liked his privacy. He was a long time in the bathroom, Lela got up to see where he was and before

Elizabeth could get up she heard someone fall. It was a terrible crash that sent chairs turning over.

She called Charlie and asked, "Daddy did you fall?" He answered, "No, it's your mother." Elizabeth hurried into the living room and found Lela on the floor. She knelt beside her mother, "Are you hurt Mama?" Lela seemed not to realize where she was. Elizabeth turned the chair upright and pushed it in front of her mother, she said, "Now Mama, you catch hold of the chair and I will push you into the chair."

Lela seemed unable to help herself much; Elizabeth pushed and tugged until she finally got her mother into the chair. She went to see about Charlie. He was coming out of the bathroom. He asked what happened and Elizabeth told him something was wrong with Lela. They went back to the living room. Lela was still sitting where Elizabeth had left her. She went to her and asked her what was wrong. She seemed dazed and unable to remember what had happened. Elizabeth went to get her some water and a wet rag to wash her face. Finally she was able to get her back to bed. She fell into an exhausted sleep as soon as she lay down.

Elizabeth went back into the living room. She got Charlie some water and sat down near him. In a low voice she told her father that she was really worried about her mother, that she knew something was happening to her that really scared her.

The next day Elizabeth cleaned both houses and cooked all of them something to eat. Charlie Howard's funeral was that afternoon. Lela said she was feeling better and insisted that Elizabeth go to the funeral.

# Chapter 5

For the next two weeks, Lela seemed some better, during that time Tony and Dee came home from Texas to stay.

Elizabeth was so worried about Dee, she was sick and was so thin and pale. She did not seem able to eat anything much. She had asthma so bad that Elizabeth was afraid she would choke to death.

Both of them were so tired from the grueling school work, and the worry of getting finished up and

35

graduating and with the move back home, that they were both sick when they got back.

Lela had a bad spell that week and had to be carried to the hospital. Memorial Day was clear and cool, the doctors said Lela could come home. As they came up the driveway Lela asked Elizabeth to stop the car and let her see the tulips that were blooming around the big pine tree beside the driveway. She sat up in the car and looked out, she said, "They are so pretty, they look like a picture."

Elizabeth fixed something for them to eat. Lela asked her if she would help her take a bath. Elizabeth made ready a pan bath, but Lela said, "No, I want to get in the shower. I want to feel the water pouring over my head, I feel so dirty." Elizabeth was afraid for her to get into the shower alone, so she pulled her clothes off and got into the shower with her mother. She shampooed her hair and held her up and let the water run over her as long as Lela wanted it to. When she had her dried off, she put a soft cotton gown on her and rolled her hair, dried and combed it. She said, "Now I can rest awhile."

After she had gotten her mother to lay down to nap, she went home to check on her own house. Dee had fixed Duncan and Tony some lunch. Elizabeth was worried about Dee because she knew she was not able to do much. They discussed what they would cook for supper. As they began, Charlie called Elizabeth and said Lela was sick again. She ran across the driveway, before she got to the door she heard her mother vomiting. When she got to the bed she could not believe how she looked, her skin was bright yellow. She ran to the phone and called the hospital and had them page Dr. Shirley. It was Dr. Russell who answered the page and said Dr. Shirley had already left the hospital. Elizabeth told him what had happened and he told her to bring her mother back as fast as she could.

Elizabeth was so scared. When they got to the hospital, Dr. Russell said she would have to have an IV. He told Elizabeth not to let her have anything to eat by mouth. The days wore on, Lela became worse. Nothing they did seemed to help. Finally they asked permission to do surgery to see what was the matter. When Dr. Shirley asked Elizabeth, she told him she would have to ask her father and other family members. While they had Lela down for tests, Elizabeth went to the chapel to pray about it. When they brought Lela back from x-ray, she seemed more herself, so Elizabeth told her what Dr. Shirley had said, and asked her what she wanted to do. She said, "If they don't find out what is wrong with me, I am going to die. I am willing for them to do whatever it takes to find out and help me if they can."

One of the other girls came to stay that night, so Elizabeth went home to talk to Charlie about the surgery. He was very upset and said, "No, I don't want them to cut on her, not knowing what they are cutting for." Elizabeth let him think about it until she had supper ready and everyone ready for bed. She went to stay with her father, as they sat and talked she said "Daddy you know mama is going to die if something is not done." Tears ran down his cheeks and Elizabeth cried too. She said, "I don't want to think about that either, but it is going to happen." Finally Charlie said, "Well, if that is the only way, I guess it will have to be done."

Bonnie had been staying at the hospital all day,

everyday with Lela since she had been carried back.

Elizabeth realized it was asking a lot of Bonnie, but the other girls all had jobs, and she could not be everywhere. She had their 87-year-old father to take care of and see that he had clean clothes and something to eat. Lela and Bonnie had always been close. Since Bonnie was a tiny girl, there was a bond that she did not have with the other grand children.

The morning that they had set for the surgery, Lela went in to a coma before they could start. Elizabeth called home and told Tony to bring Charlie to the hospital to see Lela. Dee had fixed a plate of food for Elizabeth's lunch and was sending it to her. Tony helped his grandfather dress and told him to wait at the door until he could get the car turned around and bring it close to the door. As he was turning the car around he looked in the rear view mirror and saw Charlie step out onto the top step. Then it was as if he was seeing a picture in slow motion. Charlie started to step on the next step and missed it and fell all the way to the concrete walk below. Tony jumped from the car and ran to him, his glasses were lying in several pieces on the ground. As Tony got near him he said, "Is my watch broken?" Tony said, "Granddaddy, don't be worrying about your watch, you better be thinking about your glasses and that hole you knocked in your head." He got him up and into the house, got water and a rag and washed the dirt off. He noticed his hand was swelling real bad.

Elizabeth knew something was wrong when Duncan came into the hospital room. He had a plate of food and told Elizabeth to go outside and sit on the stairs and eat it. Lela had come out of the coma, and he would not say anything about where Charlie and Tony were.

When they came to get Lela to take her for tests again, Duncan went out and told Elizabeth that Charlie had fallen out the door and he believed his hand was broken. He had called Dr. Bostwick and carried his glasses by to see if he could put them back together. Elizabeth called home to talk to Tony and he said he could not get Charlie to come to the hospital. She told Tony to let her talk to him. She told him to come on over to the emergency room and let them x-ray his hand to see if it was broken. He finally said he would come.

When they got there Tony came up to Lela's room

and Elizabeth went down to see about Charlie. The Doctor said some of the bones were cracked and he wrapped it up in an elastic bandage. Elizabeth told him to give him something for pain or he would not sleep any. His knees were scraped really bad besides the other wounds he had. She knew that a fall that far would make an 87-year-old's bones hurt real bad. She asked Tony if he would stay with him that night while she stayed at the hospital with Lela. Elizabeth brought him up to the room to see Lela before they went home. She was afraid her mother would worry about his hand, but she was so bad off, she did not seem to notice it.

Lela seemed more alert after they brought her back to the room. When it started to thunder and the lightning was so bad around ten o'clock that night, Lela called Elizabeth and asked her to raise the blind so she could see the clouds.

Elizabeth did not think she could get up. She had been diagnosed with Palindromic Rheumatism in her feet and they hurt so bad and were both as red as a ripe tomato on top. As she raised the blinds, she leaned her head against the cool glass pane. In the Wal-Mart parking lot across the street from the hospital, the raindrops danced on the black pavement. The lightning lit them as if they were tears of fire. Elizabeth turned at the sound of her mother's voice, "I want you to promise me something," she was saying. "You know I will if I can, Mama." She took her hand and pulled her into the chair beside the bed. Her eyes were bright with fever and filled with tears. "I want you to promise me that you will take care of your daddy." She said, "Do you promise?" Elizabeth brushed back tears from her eyes and said, "I promise that if the Lord will give me the health and strength, that I will do my best to take care of him as long as I can." She closed her eyes and said, "Now I can rest. I do not want him to go to the nursing home, and I knew you were the only one that would take care of him." The night nurse came in with a shot and soon Lela was asleep. Elizabeth huddled on the cot as bitter tears flowed down her cheeks. She knew her mother was dying, when she had said to her, "If you will promise me to take care of him, I promise you that as long as he lives, I will be close to you." All Elizabeth could think about that night was, "What will I do with Daddy? Why couldn't he be taken and Mama left, I could manage her so much better."

The next morning when someone came to stay with Lela, Elizabeth went home to see about Charlie. Dee had gotten Duncan off to work and cooked breakfast and fixed his lunch, fed Charlie and was doing the laundry. Elizabeth worried about her, she looked so sick herself. Her asthma had been so bad since they had been home from Texas, at times she could hardly breathe.

Elizabeth was grateful for any help she could get, but she did not want Dee to be doing work that she should be doing herself with Dee so sick she could hardly hold her head up. Elizabeth stumbled through the days. If she wasn't at the hospital with Lela at night, she was spending the night with Charlie. She was never at home anymore. She did not realize then that was the way it would be for the next three years.

Elizabeth was in so much pain; she hardly knew where she was. On June 24th, Lela became much worse; the Doctors said it would not be long. All that night most of the girls were with her. Elizabeth had to come home to take care of Charlie, the next morning she cooked breakfast, got Charlie and Shawn up and dressed for the day. She expected at anytime to hear that Lela had died. Around ten o'clock Hazel came home to stay with them so Elizabeth could go to the hospital. When she arrived at the hospital, she could see that her mother's breathing was so shallow that it would not be but a few minutes. Elizabeth stood in the doorway and looked at her sisters around their mother's bed. They were all weeping. Elizabeth leaned her head against the cold metal door frame, and thought to herself, "Why did Mama have to die such a horrible death, she was always such a good mother and wife, and a good Christian woman."

Elizabeth closed her eyes, and it was as if she looked through a kaleidoscope of colors at the life her mother had lived. She could see her as a young woman in hcr thirties, always doing something for her family or friends and neighbors. She could see her working in the fields, canning and preserving food. Cleaning her house and sewing some garment for one of the kids. Elizabeth could see her taking care of the sick when there was a need in the community, and always in her kitchen cooking. In later years, she remembered how Lela would call her when she had the preacher for lunch, so she could help her cook, remembering what a difference in then and when she used to cook on a wood stove for the preacher's family, get up and go to church in a wagon. As the years passed, they had gradually changed places, Elizabeth had become the mother and Lela and Charlie had become the children. All these things passed through Elizabeth's thoughts as she stood with tears running down her cheeks and watched her mother die.

Elizabeth's friend, Ruth Dodds, came to the hospital just as Lela passed away. They stood on the walk outside the hospital as the funeral directors came for Lela. It was so hot it seemed that the pavement would melt. Dyke Sneed told Elizabeth to come later that afternoon to fix Lela's hair. Elizabeth came home and got Charlie dressed then carried him to pick out what he wanted for the funeral. Later that afternoon, as Elizabeth set her mother's hair and dried it, she asked Dyke Sneed to let her help him dress her mother.

She stood by the table her mother lay on, and combed her hair and dressed it just the way she did every week while Lela was living.

When she had finished, she asked Mr. Sneed to let her put her mother's underclothing on. Lela had asked her to please see that it was not done with just the men present. He turned to Elizabeth and said, "I know what a lady Mrs. Lela was and of course you can do it, but we will have to help you." Elizabeth kept the sheet over her mother until she had her under garments on, then she called Mr. Sneed to help her put the dress on her. When she was ready Elizabeth was pleased with the way she looked.

She got Charlie and carried him home, fixed his supper and helped him dress to go back to the funeral home that night.

# Chapter 6

The days following the funeral dragged by, it was hot, over a hundred degrees every day. Elizabeth's feet were so swollen and red with fever that she could hardly walk on them. When she walked across the driveway to Charlie's trailer, it felt as if the rocks would come through her shoe soles.

Her day started at five-thirty each morning. Duncan would come to the window where she slept in Charlie's trailer and wake her, she would get up and go across the driveway to her house, cook breakfast, fix Duncan's lunch, make their bed and wash up the dishes. She then went back to Charlie's and cooked his breakfast, made the bed she slept in, and started the wash. By that time, Tony and Dee would be up and eating breakfast, then they would all go and start clearing the lot they were going to put their trailer on that they had bought from Herbert and Barbara Kidd. About nine thirty or ten if Shawn had not come up, Elizabeth went to see about him and fix him something to eat. She then had him come up and stay with Charlie, if he did not want to help them pick up limbs from the trees that had been cut.

Elizabeth worried about Dee, she insisted on helping clear the lot; she picked up limbs and piled them to be burned. Around noon, they came to the house and fixed lunch for all of them. The days passed, each one hotter and drier that the last. When the lot was cleared and the mobile home set up, Dee and Elizabeth started to clean it to get ready for them to move in. On the day the men from the power company came to turn on the electricity, it was around one hundred and ten degrees. They kept coming to the door for water, so finally Dee and Elizabeth made lots of iced tea, and asked them all in for a glass. They gathered in the kitchen, just thankful to be in an air- conditioned place for a few minutes. They drank over a gallon of tea. The summer dragged on, a cloud would gather, it would thunder and lightning, but it never rained a drop. The garden plants all died. There was nothing made at all. Elizabeth took bed sheets and covered the tomato plants on the hottest days to keep them from cooking in the hot sun. They ran water around them to have a few to eat. Tony looked for a job everywhere and Dee had put in her application at all the schools in the county. In September the Bank of Mississippi called Tony to work and in October, Northeast Community College called Dee to teach English. Finally things were beginning to look up for them.

When it turned cooler, Elizabeth took Charlie to Tupelo to pick out a tomb rock for Lela's grave. He looked a long time before he found the one he wanted. Mr. Carter called Elizabeth on the day they did the engraving. He wanted Charlie to come see if it was like he wanted. When they arrived they had the rock ready and sand blasting. They stopped so Charlie could see if it was like he wanted. Elizabeth had to turn her back so Charlie could not see the tears that sprang to her eyes, as she watched him trace the path to the cottage door, with the lettering, *"We shall meet again"*, that was engraved onto the face of the rock.

She gave him time to look at the rock all he wanted, then asked if it was pleasing to him. When he assured her it was just what he wanted, she got her checkbook and paid for it from her account. Mr. Carter said he would call on the day they put it up, and they could meet them at the cemetery. On the day he called it was cloudy with a cold wind from the north. Elizabeth told Charlie she did not think he should get out and stand in the cold wind while they erected the stone. Tears came to his eyes as he looked accusingly at her, "But you promised we would go." Elizabeth replied, "Well, get your coat and hat and that wool scarf and we will be off as soon as I can get my coat and car keys."

It was a long way to the cemetery, and the men had already set the base of the stone when they arrived. Elizabeth helped her father pick his way across the cemetery, stopping a little way off, so they would not be in the way of the truck that lifted the stone in place. Elizabeth wrapped the scarf around Charlie's ears and neck, so the cold wind wouldn't get to them. When the stone was set, and the men gone, they walked to the grave. Charlie stood a long time looking at the stone, Elizabeth was busy with the flowers she had brought to put on her mother's grave. Charlie turned to her as she knelt next to the stone and said, "Sis, I want you to promise me something. After I am gone, don't put any flowers on my grave, if you can't put some on Mammy and Pappy's."

Elizabeth looked up at her father and said, "I promise I will put flowers out for them as long as I can put them out for you and Mama."

Time seemed to drag along, not many of the family visited often. It seemed that when Lela died, they lost interest in Charlie. One day Elizabeth went to get her hair cut, Charlie said he did not want to go with her and she did not like leaving him alone, but she knew she would not be gone long. She was home in about an hour. Before she could get the car stopped, Charlie was at the door calling her. She hurried across to see what the matter was. Charlie was shaking and very upset. He said a federal marshal from Texas was looking for Tony. Charlie was nearly in tears, he said, "Sis, a Federal Marshal don't come looking for you unless you have done something bad." Elizabeth almost laughed as she told Charlie, "I don't know what this is about, but I know Tony has not done anything wrong, so just calm down and I will go call Tony at work and see what is going on."

The phone was ringing as Elizabeth unlocked the door. It was Tony. She told him she was just about to call him, to see what was wrong. He said while he was working in the lab in Texas, a young woman was raped and beaten. He had been on duty that night, so he was the one that examined what they took from the crime scene.

Now, he was going to go back to testify at the trial. Elizabeth told him she would gather the things he would need and have them ready when he got home. She told him she had to go and tell his grandfather what the marshal wanted, because he was about ready to have a nervous breakdown. Charlie had the door opened by the time she got there, she told him what had happened, and that she needed to go to town to get a few things Tony would need.

She told him to get his coat and he could ride with her to town. He had been so upset she did not want to go and leave him alone again.

Elizabeth's feet were still so swollen and red that at times she did not think she could walk on them all day. One day she was cleaning the trailer, she was in the back bedroom, and she was hurting so bad she did not think she could stand it. Her heart was so heavy; she just knelt by the bed and started praying. "Dear God, my feet hurt so bad, if you don't do something to help me, I'm afraid I am going to get so I can't walk and I won't be able to take care of Daddy." All at once, the lid on Lela's little music box, which sat on the dresser, flew up and the little dancer began to whirl around to the music. Elizabeth raised her head in wonder, the scent of Lela's powder and cologne were so strong in the room it almost made her sick. She couldn't understand where the odor was coming from, since none of her mother's cosmetics had been there in several months. She got to her feet and looked at the music box, the little dancer was still whirling around. When she tried to close it, it snapped open again. She picked it up and closed the lid and held it shut. As she held it she said, "Mama I know you are trying to tell me that you are close by and that you are watching over me, just like you said you would, if I would take care of daddy." All at once, a peace came over her, a well being that she had not felt since her mother got sick. She hurriedly finished cleaning the room and went to start Charlie's lunch.

# Chapter 7

The weather had turned cooler, Elizabeth couldn't believe it when the swelling in her feet went down, then the pain was not so bad. She knew it was an answer to her prayer. When she told the pastor of her church about the music box and her prayer, he looked at her as if she had suddenly sprouted another head. He started talking about people hearing and seeing things that were not there, when you were upset. Elizabeth looked at him and said, "Well, did Jesus not tell us to pray in faith and ask and it would be granted according to God's will? That's all I did." Elizabeth never tried to tell him of the many times during the next three years that God did indeed answer her prayers and sometimes he even answered before she had time to ask. That was when her faith was strengthened the most.

One day she went to clean the trailer and fix Charlie's lunch, it was around the first of December. She worked around the kitchen and cleaned the bathroom. When she finished, she went into the living room and sat down to talk to Charlie. All at once, she looked at her father and tears were running down his face. When she asked what was wrong, he said, "Sis, are we not going to have any Christmas this year?" Elizabeth had not thought that he would want to have any decorations or any reminders of how Lela always fixed for Christmas. She said, "We will if you want to." So she went right then and got the Christmas things her mother always put around the house. She put the wreath on the front door, and all the candles around the tables, and Lela's small tree on top of the television.

When she had finished, she sat down once more to talk to her father. He said, "Sis, Lela would want us to have Christmas, wouldn't she?" Elizabeth said, "Yes,

Daddy, Mama would want us to be as happy as we could be. She would want us to go on as best we could without her."

The next week, Elizabeth decorated her tree. Shawn was still small and she wanted him to enjoy Christmas as much as he could, and not see how sad they all were since Lela died. Tony and Dee came for Christmas and brought Buck the dog and everyone tried to have a good time. At least Shawn seemed happy. He sat on the floor and played with Buck.

Time passed slowly, but finally spring came. Elizabeth worked in the garden and yard, and kept both houses up. Canning season was busy and Elizabeth worked from first light until midnight to keep up with everything. Around the middle of July, one morning she was cleaning Charlie's house. She was stripping the bed to wash when she noticed the sheets were speckled with blood. She went into the living room and sat down. Charlie was eating his breakfast and she said, "Daddy, do you have a sore on you that I do not know about?" He said, "No, Sis." She asked, "Then where is that blood coming from that is all over the sheets?" Elizabeth sat frozen with dread when he said it was coming from his kidneys. She said, "We are going to the doctor as soon as I can get you an appointment."

In the next few days they went to see Dr. Shirley, when he finished examining Charlie, he came out into the hall where Elizabeth was waiting. The look on his face told Elizabeth the news was not good.

He said, "I feel a knot in the bladder area, I want you to take him to see Dr. Evans in Tupelo." He made the appointment and Elizabeth took Charlie the next day. Dr. Evans wanted him to go into the hospital for the test to see what was wrong.

The next day Elizabeth waited alone in the room for Dr. Evans to come and tell her what he found. As soon as she saw his face she knew the worst had happened. He sat down next to her and took her hand. "There is a growth in Mr. Charlie's bladder and it's probably malignant," he said. "We will have to operate as soon as we can." Elizabeth swallowed her tears and said, "But doctor, he is so old and frail, can he live through surgery of that type?" "We have no choice, it will grow so large, it will block the bladder and his kidneys will fail," he said, "You decide what you want to do." Elizabeth said, "My daddy is not senile, he will decide for himself what he wants done." He said, "I will be back when he gets through with all the tests to talk to him." That afternoon late, he came to the room. After he had told Charlie what needed to be done, Charlie turned to Elizabeth and asked, "Sis, what should I do?" She said, "Daddy that's up to you, we are going to do whatever you want done." He said, "Well, doctor, if it has to be, let's get it done."

The surgery was set for the next day, July 25, 1981.The other girls came the next morning. It seemed to take forever, when Dr. Evans came to the room to talk to them after the surgery was over, he said, "I did the best I could, but I am sorry to tell you, he will be an invalid if he makes it, he is so old and frail I couldn't get it all." One of the girls said, "We may have to put him in the nursing home, if we can't take care of him." Elizabeth stood up and said, "We are not going to put him anywhere except in his home. For fourteen months none of you have even asked if he had clean clothes or if he needed something cooked, it was as if he did not belong to any of you, well, he does, he belongs to all of us, and I am going to take care of him and all of you are going to help me."

Silence fell on the group, as Elizabeth stopped talking, she turned toward them again and said, "What do you think Mama would say to us if she could hear you talking like that. I know it will be hard to do, but if we all work together, we can do this. I'll take the most of it like I have been doing. There are four of you, one of you can come on the weekend and stay. That means you will only have one weekend a month, surely you can spare that much time for the man that took care of you when you couldn't take care of yourselves." Elizabeth could tell by the stony look on some of their faces that they did not like what she said. She also remembered the 5th Commandment. "Honor thy father and thy mother, that thy days may be long upon the land which the Lord thy God giveth thee." She quoted the verse to them and said, "I don't know about all of you, but to me, that means taking care of them when they can't take care of themselves."

The stay in the hospital was a nightmare. The drugs for pain made Charlie so aggressive he fought all of them, until they were all worn out. The surgery was in July and all the month of August was spent in the hospital.

Finally the first of September, Dr. Shirley came to the room late one night. He stood by the bed, he said, "Mr. Charlie, can you tell me who this is?" Charlie said, "It's Lela," the Doctor said, "No, you look at her and tell me who she is." It was as if a veil had been lifted from his eyes, he said, "It's Elizabeth." Dr. Shirley said, "Yes, that's right, now where is Mrs. Lela?" Tears ran down his cheeks but his eyes were focused for the first time since the surgery. He seemed to shrink within himself as he said, "She is dead, isn't she?" The doctor said, "Yes, that is right."

The next morning Elizabeth took him home from the hospital, he would not talk much. He seemed not to have any interest in the things around him.

Elizabeth fixed his bed, and said, "Daddy, don't you want to rest in your bed?" She helped him with his walker and walked along with him to the bed. As he rested, she fixed him something to eat. She placed the tray near him and sat talking to him. His feeble old hands shook until he could hardly hold the fork. Elizabeth could see it was such an effort for him to feed himself. She gently took a spoon and began talking to him while spooning the food into his mouth. She told him about the funny things he said and did while he was in the hospital. She told him about the night she and Bonnie were begging him to lay down and he told Bonnie if she would bend that flag pole down, he would show her that he could get up without her help. By talking to him of other things, she managed to get him to eat a fairly good supper.

Chapter 8

The days settled into a routine for Elizabeth, at five o'clock each morning, Duncan would come and knock on the bedroom window at Charlie's house where she slept. She would slip out so as not to wake Charlie and go home and cook breakfast and fix Duncan's lunch and get him off to work. She would put a load of wash in and clean her kitchen and make Duncan's bed, by that time it was time for her to see about Charlie and then go and get Shawn on the school bus. When Shawn went to school, she went back and cooked Charlie's breakfast and sat down with him while he ate and read the paper to him. When he finished eating, she cleaned that kitchen and put a load of wash in out there. While that was washing, she hung the ones out at her house, if it was a sunny day. Then it was time to clean the floors and do whatever else that had to be done that day.

If it was a day that Charlie had a doctor's appointment, she had to bathe and dress him and carry him to that. She tried to get them while Shawn was at school, so he would not come home and no one there.

The treatments were making Charlie so sick. After the fourth one, when Elizabeth brought him home he was so weak she did not think she was going to be able to get him into the house by herself. Finally by pushing and pulling as hard as she could she got him inside. They were both so worn out they had to sit down and rest.

She fixed his bed and had him to lie down. She went to her house and changed her clothes and started their supper. Duncan had come home, so he went to sit with Charlie while she got their supper ready. She had fixed Charlie's supper on a tray and was on her way to take it to him when Duncan came out the door. He told her Charlie was so sick that he did not think he could eat anything. She told Duncan to go on home and eat his supper and she would be back to eat as soon as she could. She sat the tray of food on the stove.

Charlie had gone into the bathroom. She went to see about him. He was hanging over his walker vomiting. She got a cold wet rag and washed his face, she put her arm around him and helped him walk toward his chair in the living room. When they got to the table in the kitchen, he had to sit and rest. She got him some Mountain Dew to drink. She thought that might settle his stomach.

She continued to wash his face with the cool cloth. He looked up at her and said, "Sis, I am so much trouble. Why don't you put me in the nursing home?"

She put her arm around the frail old shoulders and said, "Well, you did not put me in the orphans home when I was lots of trouble, now, we will not have this conversation again."

She helped him to his chair, and sat talking to him for a few minutes. She asked him if he could try to eat something since some of his medicine had to be taken with food. He said he would try. She fixed his tray on a low table and sat beside him. She had made chicken and dumplings for him and Shawn. She fed him a few bites as she talked to him. She told him how Shawn wanted her to stuff him a dumpling with flour, that's how he liked his fixed, he said, "Sis, I don't think I would want that flour in mine." She laughed and said, "I wouldn't either."

About nine o'clock he was feeling some better, so she went home to eat a few bites of supper. Duncan had put things away and washed the dishes for her. She got a plate and ate some cold peas with tomatoes, and drank some tea. She got Duncan's clothes ready for the next day and fixed his lunch box so it would just ready to put his lunch in for the next morning. Duncan went back to sit with Charlie until she could take a bath and get her gown on, and get things ready for the next day. This process was repeatcd five days a week every week. If Hazel helped with Charlie, Shawn stayed with Elizabeth, so she still had to do things to help him with his homework and the many things that go with taking care of a small child.

In the next few days Charlie was so sick, he did not want anything to eat. One day he looked up at Elizabeth and said, "Sis, please don't make me take any more of those old treatments.' She said, "Now, Daddy, I have never made you take the first one, if you don't want to take them, I am not going to try to make you. Your mind is clearer than mine is, you can decide for yourself if you want to take them or not." He said, "Well, I will not take another one." When they did not go for the next treatment, Dr. Evans called Elizabeth and really got on to her about it. She called Dr. Shirley and asked him how much time did one of the treatments buy anyone and he said, "About three weeks." Elizabeth said, "It is not worth it, Daddy is 88 years old and what time he has left, I don't want him to be so sick to his stomach all the time."

When the treatments were stopped, Charlie got slowly better, and one morning he asked if he could go to town that week. Elizabeth said, "If you feel like riding, we will go so you can see how things look." He had not been out of the house since the first of September and it was then, the first of December.

On the morning they were going, Elizabeth bathed him and got him dressed. As they rode along he looked out the window and said, "Sis, things sure do look different." And she said, "Well, it was the middle of summer when you went to the hospital and now it's the middle of winter."

Time passed along, Pearl or Faye came on the weekends they were supposed to come, and Hazel filled in on some weekends and holidays. Linda came on some nights during the week. The rest of the time Elizabeth took care of him day and night.

On the weekends Pearl came, Duncan always told her to bring her things and he would change her oil in her car, so she would not have to pay someone to do it for her. He always changed Hazel's for her, too.

Elizabeth always had supper ready when Pearl got there on Friday night. She always had Charlie bathed and ready for bed and his supper fixed, so all she had to do was visit with him and go to bed.

The New Year was the same as the old one had been, Elizabeth kept to the same schedule and tried to keep everyone going.

That spring Charlie wanted to go see his old friend Max Kidd. Elizabeth picked a sunny warm day. Max had suffered a stroke and was not able to get out of his house. Max's son Herbert, pushed his wheel chair onto the front porch, Charlie couldn't get into Max's house, so they put a chair in the yard next to the porch so they could see each other and talk. Herbert and Elizabeth went into the kitchen and she helped him wash the dishes and start lunch.

They talked about how their dads had been friends since they could remember. They walked to the door and they could hear Charlie and Max talking and both were crying. They went back to the kitchen and they both cried, too.

It seemed to do Charlie a lot of good to see his old friend, that night he talked a lot about the times they had working, fishing, and all the jokes they pulled on each other over the years. As long as she was able, Elizabeth carried him to see Max and she and Herbert would put them where they could see each other and talk. It made everyone happy.

On Charlie's birthday that year, Hazel got him a birthday cake and Elizabeth made ice cream. Shawn wanted to have a party. He said granddaddy was so old he had lots of candles to blow out.

That spring they had lots of strawberries. All Charlie wanted for lunch was a bowl of strawberries and cake. Elizabeth tried to keep pound cake made all the time to eat with his berries.

That summer Duncan caught a lot of fish out of his pond. When he had them that was all Charlie wanted for his supper. If they were big enough, she would fillet them, if not, she would help him pick the bones out.

One night they were sitting talking, all at once Charlie's eyes filled with tears. Elizabeth asked him what was wrong? He said, "Sis, you all have been so good to me, I don't know what I would have done if it hadn't been for you and Duncan." Elizabeth said, "Well, I promised Mama that as long as I could, I would take care of you. I have done my best to keep my promise."

One day the pastor of Elizabeth's church came to Visit them. It was late in the afternoon; she had just started to give Charlie a bath. She asked the pastor to sit in the living room and read until she could finish.

When she had finished and had Charlie settled in his chair, he was telling the preacher about his time in the service during the First World War. Reverend Varnon was so interested; Elizabeth excused herself and went to her house to cook their supper. When she had supper ready she fixed Charlie's tray and took it to him. They were still talking. Bro. Jim jumped up and said, "My, I didn't realize it was so late. I was enjoying this so much."

Elizabeth fixed the tray and turned the evening news on for him. She walked out with Brother Jim as he left. When they got to his car he turned to Elizabeth and said, "I guess I never realized how much work it took to care for someone sick like your dad." Elizabeth said, "No one knows until they do it, what is involved in caring for someone."

Charlie's pastor came to visit often also. When he came, Elizabeth would go home so they could talk. She always had so much to do, she was glad for someone to come visit with Charlie, so he would not have to be alone for long.

Shawn would come to play checkers with him after

school most days. They fitted Shawn a tackle box from some of Charlie's fishing stuff.

When the New Year came, 1982, first Elizabeth started to try to get the houses in order. It was warm and sunny the first of March, so she asked Shawn to help her after school in the afternoon. They raked and burned all the leaves.

One day they had worked until almost dark, Elizabeth stopped to cook supper for all of them. She told Shawn he could play while she finished supper. She almost had Charlie's tray ready to take to him, when the phone rang. Duncan was at a store near where they were finishing a house slab, he told her it would be past nine o'clock before he could get home.

She took Charlie's tray and fixed his T.V. so he could watch his program, then she went to call Shawn for supper. When they had finished eating she told him to get on his homework. When she said that he started to cry, and said, "I need bird house for tomorrow." By then he was really getting upset, Elizabeth put her arm around him and said, "Hush now, we will fix you one. "He lifted tear-filled brown eyes to her and said, "What can you do?

You are just a woman and uncle Duncan is not here to fix it for me." Elizabeth patted him on his thin shoulders and said, "Honey, you would be surprised what I can do when I get in a tight spot." She fixed Duncan's supper to keep warm and put their dishes in to soak, she told Shawn to get the flashlight. She remembered an old birdhouse on a post in the pasture. They walked along the fence until they came to the post with the birdhouse nailed to it. She took the hammer and gently pried the small house loose from the post. She took it into the house and cleaned it good. They went to the shop and found two cans of spray paint; They sprayed the roof black and the rest of the house white. They sat it on some newspaper to dry. Elizabeth asked if he had any more homework? He said he had to do some reading, but he would need her to help him. She told him to get his bath and put on his pajamas while she went to see about granddaddy and then they would read. She went and picked up Charlie's tray, he said, "Sis, I thought you were not coming back." She told him what they had been doing, and that she had to help him with his reading.

She gave Charlie his medicine and go him some Mountain Dew to drink. She fixed his T.V. on the station he wanted to watch, and told him she would be back as soon as Duncan got home and she fixed his supper and got Shawn's homework done.

She got Shawn ready for bed and took his book and sat beside him, he read his lesson until she was sure he knew all the words. She put him to bed, he said, "Read me a story." She took the book about the ugly duckling and read it to him. His eyes grew heavy and she turned out the light and sang him a lullaby. She closed the door when she was sure he was asleep.

That summer they had a good garden. Elizabeth would go as soon as Duncan left for work to pick whatever was ready. She went then to see if Charlie was awake, if not she went to her house and took a shower and cleaned her kitchen. She then went and cooked Charlie's breakfast and cleaned his house up and put in a wash. If Shawn had stayed at home that night she would go and get him up, and bring him to her house and fix him some breakfast, then she would start on the vegetables to be canned or frozen.

There was a good fig crop that year. Fig preserves were Charlie's favorite. Elizabeth wanted to make sure he had enough to have them every morning for breakfast for a year. She also made some for Duncan's father since it was his favorite, too. His mother's mind was not as good so she had forgotten how to make them. She was glad when all the vegetables and fruit were put up for the winter. In October she cleaned both houses and washed all the quilts and curtains and scrubbed both places good for the coming winter.

Bonnie had married and moved to Tupelo, she came once or twice a week and sat with Charlie so Elizabeth could do things that needed to be done at her house.

Brenda, Grant, and Lela came often to visit. Charlie looked forward to their visits. He enjoyed talking to Grant. Elizabeth always cooked a big meal for them, because Grant enjoyed eating at her house.

That Christmas Elizabeth invited all the family for Christmas dinner, she cooked almost all night the night before and was up by daylight cooking again. She tried to keep up the tradition her mother started, and she knew

Charlie wanted her to do it too. The new year started very much like the old one for Elizabeth, in January she took the flu, for the first time in the years since her mother had died, she was too sick to get up. Duncan stayed home from work, and tried to fix Charlie some-thing to eat, and gave him a bath and shave. Pearl called and Duncan told her how sick Elizabeth was, she said she would come and stay until she could get up again. That was on Friday, by Sunday night Elizabeth got up so Pearl could go home, and be at her job on Monday.

She was still so weak and dizzy she could hardly stand. She was wet with sweat and shaking so badly she had to sit down. That night, every time she had to get up to get Charlie something, she had to hold to the wall. When she got out of the bed, she had a rigor. By sheer force of will, she stayed on her feet, and kept going. It was two wecks before she could walk without holding to the wall.

# Chapter 9

One morning Elizabeth noticed blood on Charlie's nightshirt, when she asked him he said he had been bleeding for several days. She called the Doctor. They put him back in the hospital and ran tests. The doctor said the tumors were back and quite large. He wanted to start chemo again, but Charlie said no, he was not going to have any more chemo. Dr. Evans told Elizabeth she was to blame, she should have made him finish the first round of chemo and this might not have happened. Elizabeth looked at the Doctor and said, "Sir, my father will be 90 years old in March, he is not senile, if he wants to take the chemo, I will see that he gets it, but, I want you to know, that I could not make him do anything the last time he was taking it and I can't make him do anything now."

When spring holidays started at school, Shawn wanted to build a tree house in the pasture, near the pond. Duncan had given him some old lumber and nails to work with. One morning he was working on his house and Elizabeth was cleaning up Charlie's house. She was putting clothes in to wash when she heard Shawn crying, he ran in and held his hand out for Elizabeth to see. He had mashed the nail off, and burst the flesh. She was afraid he had broken the bone. She had to get him calmed down enough to let her examine it. She took a small plastic dish and filled it with alcohol, she talked him into putting his finger down in it. She told him they had to first get the dirt off before they could see how bad it was. The feeling had not come back to it, so he couldn't feel the sting the alcohol caused. When the dirt was soaked loose, Elizabeth examined it. She could see enough that she did not think the bone was broken. She took him out to her house and washed him up and put antibiotic ointment on his finger and bandaged it up. By then the feeling was coming back to it. He started crying so she gave him some Tylenol, and kissed it a lot and fixed him a bed on the couch. She turned on the cartoons, and it was not long until he was watching them. He was still in a bad way with his finger. Elizabeth had to wait on him all day that day.

When Charlie's birthday came on the 21st of March, they had a small birthday party for him. Hazel bought a birthday cake, and they let Shawn put the candles on it. He liked to blow out candles, so Charlie let him light them then they sang "Happy Birthday." He let Shawn blow them all out.

One day Elizabeth had fixed Charlie's lunch and when he finished eating he lay down for a nap. While he was asleep, she went to her house to do some things toward supper. When she went back to see about him he was awake, and sitting in his chair in the living room. She sat down to talk awhile. He said, "Sis, I have been clearing new ground. Pappy was pulling up stumps with "Prince", so we could have another tobacco patch."

He sat and tears ran down his face, he said, "I saw Pappy as plain as I ever did. Sis, it won't be long now, for he was calling me." Elizabeth could not help the tears that sprang to her eyes, she said, "Daddy are you ready to see them again?" He said, "Yes, Sis, I am."

The next week or so found him much worse. He had to be carried to the hospital and a catheter put in to drain his bladder.

# Chapter 10

From that time on, he seemed to worsen every day. One Friday night, when Pearl had come for the weekend, he was much worse, she called Elizabeth way in the night to come over. As they worked over him trying to do something to make him more comfortable, Elizabeth said to Pearl, "This is the worst thing." Pearl said, "No, it could be worse." Elizabeth said, "Well, what could be worse?" Pearl said, "Mama could be living, can you imagine what we would do with her? She would be beside herself, and we could not do what she would want done, so she would be in worse shape." Elizabeth said,

"Yes, you are right, she always wanted the best for Daddy." From that time on there was no sleeping at night, for Charlie hurt so bad he could not rest. Elizabeth never knew what it was like to get more than an hour some nights. By the time one of them would come on Friday night, her head would be so light she could hardly walk. She felt like she was floating about two feet off the ground, and her eyes would not focus on anything she was so tired. One morning everyone was gone to work, Elizabeth went to see about Charlie and he said, "Sis, I am hurting so bad." She looked and the catheter was not draining. She got a pan and she emptied it. Sure enough, nothing was coming through. She looked and it seemed to her she could see his stomach swelling. She said, "Daddy, why did you wait until everyone was gone, I may not be able to find someone to help me get you into the car to go to the hospital." She called everyone she could think of, but no one was home. She finally thought of the mailman. She knew he would be along about nine o'clock and she knew he would help her get Charlie into the car.

She bathed and dressed him and packed his bag. She ran home and took a quick shower and dressed. She got everything ready and locked her house, turned the car around and got Charlie's bag and put it in the car and went to wait. Mr. Hall came promptly at 9 o'clock. Elizabeth went out and explained the situation to him. He was glad to help her, so finally they were on their way to the hospital.

It was that way from then on. One night Charlie had been especially restless, Elizabeth worked until well after midnight trying to find something that would make him a little more comfortable. When she thought he was asleep, she went to her bedroom. She felt that she just had to stretch out and close her eyes for a few minutes. Sometime later she awoke to heavy footsteps coming toward her bedroom.

She was so frightened, all she could think of was to get the gun to protect them. She thought Charlie had managed to get up and open the door. She feared someone was coming in to do them some harm. All at once, a calm came over her. She seemed to lose the will to sit up on the bedside. A force of some kind seemed to push her down on the pillow. It seemed she could feel a hand smoothing her hair back from her forehead and the sheet being smoothed over her. She lay like that, at peace for a few minutes, before she remembered Charlie. She got out of bed, no longer afraid, and went toward Charlie's room. When she walked up to the bed, she saw that his eyes were open. She said, "Daddy, do you want something?" He said, "I would like a cup of Mountain Dew." She got his drink and took it to the room and raised his head. He looked up at her and asked, "Sis, did you see your mama?" She said, "No, Daddy." He said, "Well, I don't know why you did not, she was standing right by the window there when you came in the room."

Elizabeth looked but all she saw was the breeze from the air conditioner blowing the curtain. He seemed upset because she would not say she had seen Lela, she said, "Daddy, if you saw her that is good enough for me." She said, "I was asleep, but someone walking woke me up." Elizabeth walked over to the window. The scent of Lela's powder was so strong. She knew when she smelled it that Charlie had been visited by her mother's spirit. She remembered what her mother had said to her that last night in the hospital, "If you take care of your daddy, I will always be close to you as long as he lives." Elizabeth said, "Daddy, maybe we should not tell anyone what has happened tonight. We know what happened, but to people that has never had this happen to them, they will think we have gone off our rocker." Elizabeth sat with him while he drank his drink, he told her it would not be long now. She did not try to tell him otherwise, she felt that he was right. She sat in the chair pulled up by his hospital bed and rested her forehead on the cool rails. She asked him if he wanted to tell her what he wanted done. He said, "Sis, first I want to tell you how much I appreciate what you have done for your mother and me." Elizabeth sat with bowed head, listening to what he said; she had never heard her father talk like that to anyone. He said, "I know how hard it has been for you, lots of times. When I decided to sell the old home place, I knew that if you did not take us in, we would not have anywhere to go. I know some of the others would tell us we could move with them, but I also knew that the next day they might be moved somewhere else. I knew your home was the most stable of the bunch, that's why we wanted to move here."

He went on, "I knew that whatever Duncan told me, that would be the way it would be. You have a good husband, Sis, and he has been like a son to us." I said, "He loved you and Mama, I think he has shown that." He said, "You keep taking care of Shawn, I don't know what they would have done if you had not helped them out." I said, "Don't worry Daddy, you know I will always do that as long as I can." I said, "Why do you worry about him?" He said, "He is the only little one we have now and his daddy don't seem to care what happens to him, so I want you to promise me you will look out for him." I took the cup and sat it on the bedside table, and said, "I promise I will look out for him."

"I feel like I can rest now," he said. The pain medicine did not help much anymore; Elizabeth could see the pain on her father's face. He never slept any except brief naps.

One night toward the middle of June, everyone had gone to bed except Charlie and Elizabeth. He was in so much pain he could not lay down. He said, "Sis, Hailey's Comet is going to visible tonight. The last time I saw it was 1910; I was seventeen years old. I never thought I would live to see it again. Do you think we can go out on the porch and see it?" Elizabeth wanted him to be able to see the comet again, so she went to her house and got the binoculars.

She took a chair and fixed it so he could sit and maybe see the comet. She was almost afraid to take him out and no one awake except them, but she was not going to let him miss this if she could help it. She helped him up on his walker, and they got to the chair on the porch. She took the binoculars and set them just right, she held them out so he could put them on. He was so excited, he said, "Sis, I see it! I can really see it!" Elizabeth let him sit as long as he wanted and look at the comet. When they were back in the house, he wanted to sit in his chair and talk. Elizabeth sat in her mother's chair and put her feet up while Charlie told her about the first time he saw the comet. He told her people thought the end of the world was coming; it was so big and bright. He wanted to tell her about going to Detroit and working in a car factory. He said he worked where the wheels were made, he said the spokes were made out of wood at that time. They sat talking for a long time, he told her a story of one of his mother's sisters that Elizabeth never knew about. He said this aunt of his was the youngest of the family, and his Grandmother Simmons was staying with her on this particular day. It had snowed the night before and Pappy had to go to town. As he was coming home he saw Grandma Simmons walking toward Latham. When he stopped the wagon and helped her into it, she told him that her daughter had told her to leave. Pappy was so mad when they got home he called Mammy and told her to take care of her mother. Once Grandma Simmons was seated by the fire, Pappy told Mammy that her sister's name would never be mentioned in his house again.

Elizabeth asked, "What was her name?" Charlie said, "I don't know, Sis, I was only four years old and after that day, her name was never called in our house."

The cuckoo clock on the wall said 1a.m. Elizabeth said, "Daddy do you want to lay down?" He said, "I know you are tired, but I am not sleepy yet." Elizabeth sat back down, and said, "Well, you tell me when you are ready to go to bed."

They talked until the cuckoo said 2 a.m. Charlie said, "Sis, we better lay down, you won't be able to get up in the morning." Elizabeth wondered how she would be able to do what she had to do the next day, knowing all the time she had no choice, that when five o'clock came, she would have to hit the floor, and start another day.

The strawberries were ready to pick the next morning, but Charlie had taken worse and Elizabeth could not pick them for she had to do something for him all day. The pain had gotten much worse. Elizabeth called the Doctor and he sent more pain medicine. Late that afternoon he began to feel some better. Duncan came home from work and Elizabeth had everything done so they could eat supper. When she fed Charlie and cleaned that kitchen, she told Duncan to sit with him and she would pick the strawberries. She looked at her garden and she could see the beans were growing fast and she knew that they would be ready to can in another week or two. She wondered how she would do all she had to do, and every day she could see Charlie getting worse.

That Saturday Grant, Brenda, and Lela came to spend the night.

Elizabeth gathered fresh vegetables from the garden, and cooked a big meal. Grant liked to eat with her, and she always tried to cook a good meal for him. He had brought the slides from their vacation in Florida, two weeks before. He wanted Charlie to see them. After supper he set the projector up and got things ready, while Elizabeth and Brenda washed the dishes and cleaned the kitchen. They all gathered and watched the pictures of little Lela as she frolicked in the waves at Fort Walton Beach. Charlie enjoyed seeing the sand and waves as they came crashing onto the beach. Grant and Lela played with a green striped beach ball, until the waves carried it out too far to catch.

Grant and Brenda wanted to stay the night with Charlie. Elizabeth told Brenda what to expect. Grant said he would get up with him and see that he had what he needed. Elizabeth told them if they needed her to ring the bell and she would be there in a few minutes. Duncan had gone to Boy Scout camp with Shawn to spend the night. Elizabeth told Lela she could spend the night with her, so they went to her house. They sat and talked for a while, then Lela watched television until bedtime. Elizabeth took a long bath and lay down, it seemed that she had just closed her eyes, when the doorbell jarred her awake. She knew that something had happened, so she slipped into a robe and ran across the driveway. Grant met her at the door, he said, "Granddaddy is bleeding, it is all over the bed." When Elizabeth turned back the covers, she could see what had scared them so much. The catheter had gotten stopped up and blood was seeping back through the end of it and onto the bed. She told Brenda to get her a pan of warm water and a rag.

She had to irrigate the catheter and get the blood clot out, then wash it out, bathe Charlie, and change the bed. When she had finished she went back to her house, Lela was still sleeping, she never knew Elizabeth was not there for that while.

The week started off as usual, everyone went to work, and Shawn stayed with Charlie a lot and they would play checkers, if Charlie was able. Monday night the pain was so bad Charlie did not sleep any, the medicine was not strong enough to dull the pain, but a few minutes at a time. Elizabeth knew that he was getting much worse, all day Tuesday he hurt so bad, Elizabeth did not have time to do anything, except try to do something that would make him a little more comfortable. When she finished supper, and everyone was settled for the night, she could see Charlie was more swollen, his fingers looked like they were twice the size they should be. She gave him a pain pill and sat in the living room. He dozed for a few minutes, and then he was groaning with pain again. She got him some Mountain Dew to drink, and sat by his bed. They talked about the family and other things. When the cuckoo clock said two o'clock, Charlie said, "Sis, you go lay down, I know you are give out." Elizabeth knew that time was running out, she said, "I am going to stay here." He said, "You can't do any more for me, my time is up." Elizabeth lay her head on the cool bars of the hospital bed, and said, "Well, I can be with you, Mama would want me to stay."

She reached and took his hand, and sat holding it. She felt that he needed someone to hang onto at that time, knowing his life was almost over. He talked about his life, he said, "Sis, I guess I have lived in the time period that more has happened than any other time in history." He continued talking, "I can remember the first car that was made, all the new medicine that has helped so many people. I saw a man walk on the moon. All of this in 90 years." He went on talking, "I want you to get the boys to be pall bearers for me." "Who do you want?" she asked. "I want Tony and Grant, Mike and Mitchell, one of Pearl's boys or one of the girl's husbands, and Hayes Howard. I want Shawn to walk behind my casket, I know he is not big enough to be a pall bearer, but I want him to walk and sit with the other boys."

Elizabeth patted his hand and said, "I will see that it is done just like you want it or as near as it can be." "What else do you want done?" He told her he wanted a flag-draped casket and Rev. Bullock to do his service. She promised him that all would be as he wanted. He said, "Sis, I don't want you to worry about anything, no one could have done more for their parents than you have." She said, "Well, Daddy, you know who my example was, you and Mama. Everyday of my growing up years, I saw how you took care of your parents. Children learn by example. I was blessed to have a Christian mother and daddy as my example." Elizabeth could see the pain on his face. She got another pain pill and some water for him.

When she turned the light on, she could see he was even more swollen. She said, "Daddy, I think I ought to call the ambulance. I think you are going to need to go to the hospital." He said, "Yes, Sis, I think I am. These pills won't seem to ease me anymore." Elizabeth started to go make the call; she noticed the streaks of pink in the east. She had not noticed that it was five o'clock and almost daybreak. When she got to her house, Duncan was just getting up, she told him that she thought Charlie should go to the hospital. She washed up and put on some clothes and made the call.

When the ambulance came, Hazel came up and wanted to go to the hospital with him, so Elizabeth told her she would come later. The EMTs came in with the stretcher and placed Charlie on it, they started out the door. As they got to the place where he could see Lela's picture that was hanging on the wall, just as you went out the door, He said, "Wait boys." The men stopped and he lay looking at her picture for a long moment. It was if he knew he would never be back again.

Elizabeth stood in the door with tears in her eyes and watched the red tail lights of the ambulance until it pulled onto the highway. She went to her house and cooked breakfast, and got Duncan off to work. She went to Hazel's house and got Shawn up and brought him to her house and fixed his breakfast. She bathed and dressed and got Shawn ready and they went to the hospital. By that time, Pearl had come. She had had surgery six weeks before and had not been able to stay with Charlie since. She wanted to sit with him so, Elizabeth took Shawn and went home.

Now that he was in the hospital, one of them wanted to stay with him, so Elizabeth stayed home and tried to catch up on some of the work that she had not had time to do.

The next day, Linda called and wanted her to come to the hospital to give Charlie a bath. She told Shawn to get ready; they had to go see Granddaddy. He did not want to stay at the hospital, but she told him they had to because there was no one else to stay. Linda wanted to stay that night, Pearl wanted to stay the next night, Faye was going to stay on Thursday. That Thursday morning when Duncan left for work, Elizabeth got Shawn to go back to sleep and she lay back down too. She was so tired from the many months of staying awake, most all time, she felt she just had to sleep some. Around eleven o'clock the phone woke her, Linda said, "Daddy has just died and Dr. Shirley wants to see you."

When she got there, everyone had left the room. She walked up to the bed and looked down at Charlie. She said, "Daddy, as the Apostle Paul said in the Bible, *'You have fought the good fight, you have finished your course, your time has come to be offered, and the time of your departure is here.'* Rest now, and I will, too."

She turned as the Doctor entered the room and said, "I asked you to come, because, I wanted to tell you that I have never seen anyone take any better care of their parents than you have. You could lay down in the parking lot and go to sleep as far as worrying about anything, because a clear conscience makes a soft pillow."

Elizabeth said, "I want you to know how much I appreciate you for always being so kind to them. Most Doctors don't have time for old people, but you always seemed to care and for that I thank you." She watched as the doctor wrote out the death certificate. She had not noticed the date was June 30, 1983. She asked if he remembered that Lela had died June 25, 1980. He said, "I knew it was close to the same time." The funeral was Saturday morning. She planned it just as Charlie had wanted. The flag draped casket, the grandsons as pallbearers and Reverend Bullock and Reverend Varnon to do the service. At the grave site, she stood looking at all the flowers, so many they made a blanket for Lela's, Mammy and Pappy's and Thomas' grave. The ladies of Elizabeth's church had brought in lots of food. She invited all of them to eat lunch after the funeral.

The years passed, but the memories lingered.

Elizabeth sat one day looking at the picture album. As she turned the pages, the smiling faces looked out at her, she could see Bonnie in Lela's wedding picture. She could see the set of Charlie's jaw in the picture of Miles. On the next page was Lela's brother, Frank, his smiling gray eyes were the same as Mike's The picture of her grandfather, Henry, was just like looking at her son, Tony. He stood with his thumbs hooked in his pockets just like Henry always did.

As she looked at all the beloved faces, of the ones that had gone before, she thought, it is so true. "The scroll of life does unroll for us to see our loved ones that live on in memory."

99

# Acknowledgements

Thanks, of course, **Mable Elizabeth Gates** for putting these memories on paper. This gift to our family (and any reader) is one that can't be compared to any tangible thing because these details would otherwise have been lost to the ages.

Special thanks to Aunt Mable's niece, my mom, **Brenda Bell** for lovingly re-typing these pages from the original type-written manuscript, keeping me on track, and supporting the project.

Thank you to my husband, **Mike Hartsaw**, for putting up with me sitting at the computer hour upon hour to work on this project. It means so much to know he understands.

If you haven't read the first book, be sure to order your copy today.

COMING SOON...
*A special collection of several original stories by Mable Elizabeth Gates—featuring (with permission) a touching short story published by The University of Mississippi in a 1984 book entitled, Memories of Mississippi.*

BONUS: Lost family recipes, including Lela's famous biscuits and selections from each of the siblings.